mummer

prisoner

scavenger

thief

mummer

prisoner

scavenger

thief

Poems

CHRIS RANSICK

CONUN
DRUM
PRESS

AN IMPRINT OF BOWER HOUSE

DENVER

Library of Congress Control Number: 2019938020

ISBN: 978-1-942280-63-7

10 9 8 7 6 5 4 3 2 1

Acknowledgments

Some of these poems have appeared in existing or previous versions in the following journals and as collaborations or installations, as noted. "Canoe Canoe" and "Crow and Bone" *Mountain Gazette*; "The Sand Road," "Nameless Tarn," and "Your River Has a Beautiful Town" *Sage Green Journal*; "Oil and Water" *Colorado Independent*; "Mano 94.002.18" Manual Labors, a 2007 collaborative exhibit at The Lab, Denver; "Passion, There" Love, a Joint Venture, a 2009 collaboration with Ballet Nouveau Colorado; "New Sugar" Love in the Digital Age, a 2012 collaboration with Ballet Nouveau Colorado; "Four Turns Counterclockwise," a 2013 ekphrastic collaboration with Jeffrey Wenzel & Art Students League of Denver.

My thanks go to Michael Henry whose care and handling of the manuscript in development was invaluable.

mummer: a person acting in a masked mime

prisoner: a person trapped by a set of circumstances

scavenger: a person who collects abandoned items

thief: a person who takes things by stealth, without force
   or violence

for Steve

Table of Contents

I: mummer

II: prisoner

III: scavenger

IV: thief

Everyone can play the mummer's part, and represent an honest person on the stage; but inwardly, within his own bosom, where all is permitted us, where all is concealed, to keep a principle there, that's the point.

—Michel De Montaigne

I was fighting a small fight of my own which wasn't leading anywhere—but like a man with a bent spoon trying to dig through a cement wall I knew that a small fight was better than quitting: it kept the heart alive.

—Charles Bukowski

I

mummer

Liminal Hymnal

here is a book of songs
with words that lift like wings
your body from all wrongs

your tongue toward what it sings
here is the liminal light
the awakening it brings

lie still until your sight
sharpens and shapes emerge
out of the ocean of night

fruit on the trellised verge
hand that breaks the stem
mouth that answers the urge

listen inside the dream
for a voice that speaks the book
pulled page by page from a stream

bright trout on a hook
held in the palm caressed
released again to the brook

ushering you to your rest
telling you nothing you knew and
everything you may have guessed

Darkness and Work in the Dark

dance on the browning grass the storm's still
far off and the bear tucked back in her lair

dance though ice forms for the first time
a grey rime on pond shallows where chilled

fish stunned by the insult nudge one another
gallows humor among stiffening moss and

slick rocks under a twilit sky phasing through
blues fine as Neptune's cloak of cold methane

yes the darkness who could forget it's always
dark somewhere and yet there's the work

in the dark the welcome we nightly offer
by which and from which we raise ourselves

Elm Street

1

calm except for crows'
occasional caws

parting remarks
about broken things

corvid grief sung rough
among sun-teased leaves

even as sirens insist
there's still a chance

to chase a loosed ghost
back into its

bent body for doctors
to whisper back together

2

jackhammer
barking cur
back door slammer
end of summer

noon the same
but dusk sooner
the crickets name
night the winner

vines spent seasons
on designs
hung so heavy
grapes to wines

3

if autumn wind blows down the elm
call it cruel and hide inside cower
in the cellar in a coward's realm
far from wind blowing down the elm
where light won't come where fear's a film
coating the clock slowing the hour
while fierce wind blows down the elm
and leaves a gouge where there was a tower

pray to a ghost who hears no pleas
seasonal ritual stripped of meaning
tuck your head and hug your knees
pray to a god who hears no pleas
keen with the wind find harmonies
so gusts race whatever you're keening
into the distance where all longing flees
and let clouds end the prayer by raining

4

the neighbor's manic
dog stopped barking

yes it did at midnight
tiny fierce hyena of hate

ceased its animal angst
just like that

erased his nightmare
left at a seashore

where the moon pulled
hard at the bay and

sea lions beached
all round him

shifting to women
asleep on sand

5

trench in the earth by
fence and frosted weeds

receives a silver furred
companion and welcomes with

stones around her curled body
cold cockpit of November dirt

a purrless clawless journey
decomposing into eternity's

mouth that both sustains
and swallows us all after

dances and dreams and
thin exquisite pleasures

purchased with breath
leaving none to sing requiem

only this hummock to
haunt summers

6

let winter melt slow into spring far from summer
sun a fraction more insistent and sooner
gutter's black water glistens
when you talk to the old man he listens
words more precious as sight grows dimmer

a warm night is a cruel rumor
a cold one a hammer
waste no prayer on what you can't hasten
let winter melt slow into spring

you can almost hear snowbanks simmer
and icicles drip as scavengers stammer
mummers in the elms their talons fasten
tight on dead limbs they hurl admonitions
why hack at sheet ice you can't sunder
let winter melt slow into spring

Mother Dying

mother matrix
source and substance
from your body
came a monster
and an angel
in one package
joyful wreckage
troubled winner
humble hero
stumbling zero

we will witness
your declension
knowing nothing
of this business
mother show us
what's below us
present future
past or never
first you birthed us
now you leave us

we are now lost
in a forest
lost the children
who adore us
lost the scout
who knew the route
gone the moon
dry the well
touch the stone
hear the bell

Passion, There

where a flock of birds rushes overhead
a thousand wings flash in unison

where limbs leave their bodies before
bone and muscle rush together again

where the clasp feels the delicate signal
and after much clinging unclasps

where figures by bare trees come close
her hand on his hip unaware of all else

where she moves in pale blue light at dawn
music rustles from crimson drapes

where they share space bones vibrate
slow and deep at each caress

where they slide between vines and leaves
always hungry in a jungle teeming

where they sleep and inhabit the same dream
two crows' shadows pass mid-flight

where everyone squints at well lit paintings
these two lovers leap too close to statues

where one lover arcs like a crescent moon
the other one lies like a shark on an altar

where they stand two trees across a narrow river
tossed by wind anchored by rock

where in waves of blacktop heat she shimmers
her motions mirrored in the building's glass

where her black hair blows about them both
on the sand beside a blue-green bay

where they spin each other like silver coins
glinting glinting glinting in sun

Tornado Comes to Last Chance, Colorado

funnel take me up I'm done
drive fierce darkness over the sun

roaring wind velocity
lift my carcass transport me

over plains breached by eroded buttes
ruined farms and upturned roots

over arroyos so dry they forgot
what water is and wind is not

I'll be smarter faster one with lightning
more than a match for what I'm fighting

I renounce these dingy drapes
mornings of mud and frozen ropes

give me fierce wind with a hole inside
where surrendering men may hide

I've lived in Last Chance all my life
tilled beside my toughened wife

acres by the river snowmelt green
dreaming of places we've never seen

just beyond the banks and bend
lift her up please lift my friend

swirl her toward me spin her near
eye to eye in the eye's muted roar

chance please bring us together at last
settle us with the rest of the dust

Nihilist's Lullaby

sleep is always the best balm
for a day when the forest burns down

dreams are recompense for smoky
ruin and the death of gentle women

remember how the great blue spruce
swayed and fell when hot winds came

remember the paths where you carried her
until your arms fell empty

September sunlight slants to Earth
falls rich on the hill's south slope

where coyote sleeps in her den until dusk
tomorrow her pups are target practice

but she'll chase down a rabbit tonight
show no grief between scrub oak and

sagebrush express no remorse
for the kill and the way her prey cries

The Pain Merchant

it was never about the sound of screams
coming from down the hall
it was never about erotic dreams
sleep as you must where you will

no one comes twice to this angry planet
rippling with fires and storms
it's a B movie and you don't star dammit
having signed without reading the terms

your character dies in the final scene
the pain merchant's hands at his throat
you know where you're going but where have you been
just row row the leaking boat

what's first is lost what's now not past
forgiven by priests and made clean
the eye sees and the ear hears at last
subtle waves subterranean scenes

Imaginationman

he hikes along a creek that doesn't flow
walks up a canyon that will not echo
makes up all the things he knows

a mule amenable to heavy bags
his split hooves his back that sags
fattened on apples good grass and figs

he ditchsleeps behind the supermarket
midnight delivery doors make a racket
in such a jungle he hides in the thicket

dreams of green water white sand
the scent of exotic fruit on the wind
a sun that gently erases his mind

he sometimes forgets that he is who he's been
no longer believes in ghosts though he's seen
a mysterious man with a certain sheen

walking torn and naked in tall wet grass
what he wouldn't give if he could ask
what is the secret to living with less

2

I want a dram of whisky said
imaginationman

walking into a dangerous room
the most dangerous man of all

let's see some ID some ideas
that don't stink let's see fruit

on the goddamn tree
and behold it was so

what does it mean to behave as a man
can anyone here tell me that

he said to the assembled and
knocked back his drink and vanished

   3

he was worse than some but better than most
did his best for example with the ancient books
licked dust from his fingers to turn the pages
scared off silverfish and caressed the spines

did his best to discover the ancient books
and the wisdom within that might have been lost
scared off silverfish and caressed the spines
of girls who followed him into the stacks

and the wisdom within that might have been lost
poured over him honey of a golden hue
and the girls who followed him into the stacks
hid mysteries in their mouths those vessels

poured over him honey of a golden hue
amid those perfumes such ethereal music

and mysteries in their mouths those vessels
that later fell silent to him on the street

amid these perfumes the ethereal music
within their limbs the language he'd guessed
that later fell silent to him on the street
who was worse than some but better than most

4

two moons not just the usual one
not far to go and ready to run

he told crow and crow cawed back
all in the murder would conceal his track

he whispered to fox to show the way
to blend with weeds at the end of day

no music needed but the sound of breath
rhythm of footfalls stars as a wreath

II

prisoner

Book of Curses

1

predawn candle's feeble light
singe the moon's translucent
skin until it yields a frigid night

what is right and what is decent
fruits frost-blasted on the vine
ruins hung beyond the casement

may all sharp blades rust in rain
may ill schemes turn tongues black
pay the cruel with shiny coins

made of winces and bad luck
turn back their toxic caresses
blunt their weapons on rock

2

brown grass winter grass
two glass trees
the neighbor on his knees
sure to freeze his ass
looking for lost keys

how fast passed summer
remember sunlight
heavy on the skins of fruit
left hand on heart and a hammer
held in right

3

| tight and black | a hunk of coarse coal |
| compacted fantasies | a-throb with thrill |

memory ember aglow emitting
a noxious fume never forgetting

its dark lair the face of the jailer
each coffin nail each hand on hammer

invent at night new *Inferno* rings
where a crow feasts and a hornet stings

if you find yourself among these verses
inside a song from the furnace of curses

sung to break chains remove the veil
reveal the wound so hard to heal

burn ache tremble and burn
little ball of rage we all must own

bring me all ash to a sacred grove
leave my enemies what they deserve

4

lean out gargoyle from a
concrete cornice

spit rain and grin
in sun begrimed and

missing a tongue and done
with remonstrations

recitations of rights and
obsolete oaths

night falls and falls
each dawn between

casting low sun on your teeth
turning you to stone

5

here's a ship to sail all night
on a shallow sea of nightmares
a yellow room hung with
the skins of prisoners
will you not eat of this poem
and be nourished you will
haunt the crossroads hunt
all night and never rest

6

painmaker nausea's painter
a sirocco that parches throats
build me a castle with a dungeon tonight
build me a castle with moats

toothgrinder no soothing banishes
sleepbuster please make me humble

ignite ignored and tiny nerves
remind my flesh I'm animal

I'll make of pain a smooth stone
polished with aches and worry
hidden in my gut beside regrets
forgotten except when I'm weary

painmaker let us walk together
help me perfect my flinch
weakness leaving the body etc
tightens my tongue with a wrench

7

believe in the power of rain
to dissolve the tongues of liars
and false friends to leach pain

from wounds to banish desires
that can never be sated true
companions the invisible fires

that heat cells an impossibly blue
sky going black a star long dead
persisting as light lancing through

vast indifference through the chill void
all these inanimate things that bless
and comfort to which you are wed

know neither failure nor success
whether you wake or turn again to sleep
they make up your only house

Dead Kit Fox

elms' first spent yellows
spot the footpath fetid
scent burgeoning above

creekfunk pale weedy
perfumes car exhaust
a patch of torn fur

puddle of dried blood
scatter of twigs clawed
dirt the suggested echo

of mortality's chorus
on the tongue of fox
lolling from a grimace

once on a frigid
February morning I
spooked him on his

final foray as dawn
embarrassed again the
suburb with orange light

he froze I froze he
trotted to the post
and marked it

stared through the back
of my head a long
moment both of us

memorizing eternity
beasts in a shrunken
scab of wildness

between city streets
blessed still by hawks
rabbits mice but also

cluttered with plastic
bags cups cardboard boxes
dogshit and dross

kids had come to
poke prod and turn
the kit's carcass with sticks

his missing entrails
gnawed hindquarters
please may it be a coyote

took him not loose pets
or some loser with a
.22 and nothing to do

autumn breezes
ruffle the white tip
of magnificent tail

and me without a
sharp blade to cut it loose
and carry it home

Sunday Morning on the Corner of Lost & Forgotten

1

rain paints the plywood sheets
where windows were
and each droplet is a prayer
ignored by gods grown tired of
supplicants kneeling in filthy alleys
where yesterday's expletives
pocked the brickwork
conditional surrender sung
by people so poor even dumpsters
sit empty behind their
high narrow tenements
the rusted steps of loose-hung
fire escapes thick with
fat pigeons who won't stop
dropping two-tone insults
and cooing remonstrations at the
derelict church and they all
take flight at once
every time a gun goes off

2

if clouds part night still falls
wake late and exhaust will already
have made the morning reek
an urban religion's incense
to bless the shared space
dawn its best bet for forgiveness

3

woman conversing with her purse
walks the median between lanes
two worlds rushing at her a bus
heading back to nostalgic regret
and a truck toward what might happen
billboard depicts a sleeper dreaming
without reality to measure against
and no voice to wrestle silence
into conversation though a
clocktower bell marks the moment
eternal the now wherein she is free

Broken Girl

broken girl
whose brain won't work
won't prime the pump
cry dry the well
we sit in a concrete
box and toss stones
at walls wondering
how long this will take
you're oddly brave
to strive and strive
show me those
crazy sketches again
there are clues in the
curving lines and fierce
scribbles there are
answers in the sigils
where manias crease
cartoon faces
mad monochrome creatures
trapped in margins and
confused by their own
sudden synthesis a
cruel compression into
two dimensions
their legs dangling
over an abyss and the
lack of a sequence
to animate them toward
what they desire
which is finally nothingness
which is what they fear

Suspended Man

on a rounded rockface
under purple skies
no way up or down

blind to the hawk
to the river churning
green and white

in canyon confines
where he'd plummet
a blunt immersion in

dark muscled currents
thrilled stunned and thrashing
for far dim stars

Four Turns Counterclockwise

1

in this vortex of broken bone
find a home and be forgiven
enter the frame be whole be alone
the only truth you'll be given

you must forgive to be forgiven
walk blue streets leg dragging the trap
sometimes the truth is no kind of haven
will you never learn to read the map

walk blue streets leg dragging the trap
none of the big dogs bite I swear
turn at this corner marked on the map
it's fake blood the mannequins wear

none of the big dogs bite I swear
though their jaws make a terrible sound
fake blood on bricks in an eloquent smear
black bits of birds fall to the ground

you know what's coming from the terrible sound
uttered in language you never have known
bits of black words fall to the ground
get a bird's eye view once you've flown

learned a language you never have known
and use of wings when needed most
and a bird's eye view now that you've flown
flense your flesh and become a ghost

speak the color of truths you're given
enter the frame and be alone
find here a home and be forgiven
in this fortress of broken bone

2

limbs tumble from the dream
pile in the streets
blunted disarticulated

so measure space between
numbness and reverie
carefully by hue and shape

light paints even a
landfill at dusk
then black streets blue

mock sleep until you walk them
until you tire and finally rest
if you wake to disasters

stunned and hungry in a maze
know you made it yourself from
box shreds and body parts

surely you know all the angles
gaps gullies and dead ends
go find your way home again

3

flesh tone bleached stone gunmetal grey
first came fuchsia and later the sky

edges angles bend to breaking
box of pain with the bottom leaking

unfurled flag of a nation of rogues
concrete prowled by miscreant dogs

whatever the eye delivers the mind
blasted and blown by incessant wind

night terror nightmare night all day
make one wrong turn and lose your way

wake under barbed wire stone and stumps
somebody anybody please light the lamps

no friends in boxcars or under the bridge
and the stubborn crow's only song is a dirge

4

from on high these ruins become a river
akimbo gestures shape a story fierce
above the stage strange spirits hover
from on high these ruins become a river
there's nowhere here the eye can linger
paths will cross and sharpness pierce
from on high these ruins become a river
eloquent gestures the hue of grace

Subtropical Cyclone

grind the ocèan
milk cloud millstone

whip froth so far inland
it lands like snow

lift great maples from
sockets and flip ships

full moon pull tides high
surge and scrub clean

blacktop and bring rain
to rinse winds to

buff and polish pocked
towers of the old bridge

surely one drowned man
is sacrifice enough

to accompany the last bird
blown to oblivion

Mr. Bloodyhands Visits Planet Gun

going to the sale today on Glocks
the big bore one the one I want

bullet per second is what I seek
lot of coyotes in a pen etc

my senator my senator why hast thou
forsaken us all the people will cry

around a memorial near the freeway
yes the lobbyist was that good

in bed and the money just too green
too tender on the senator's tongue

I automatically must take
the fastest deadliest package

give it all to me give me that black
neck protection and those kevlar pants

for my ass and a gas mask and
earplugs to drown out screams

everyone will be so sad
even lovers will not make love

and fruits won't grow in
cul de sac gardens flooded with grief

can you recommend a website for
hauling down serious ammo

yes thanks please I'll pay in cash and no
I won't need the receipt

Columbine Antiphon

what would a father do
with this news what
would a mother do
> break bones in their hands
> pounding the earth break
> every oath and promise

where are the souls
of the suddenly dead
where do killers' souls go
> nowhere nowhere
> you know the place
> nowhere you can know

why does the grief of fathers pool
why do mothers hang their
shreds from a hook of silence
> their ghosts have endless
> memory and the vale
> they haunt is vast

III

scavenger

Misfortune Cookies

if you are reading this you are already lucky

next time check your dim sum carefully for stones

she doesn't love you as much as she loves Pu Pu Platter

your habit of leaving small tips will follow you to hell

the bad news is you will not be fired from your job

always bet on number 7—you'll still lose but will feel
   strangely vindicated

you just ate too much didn't you

yes the hostess sat you here on purpose

dare to dream—for you the greatest risk of all

entropy is inevitable but will now focus on you

the best time to invest your money was before

the one you fantasize about cannot remember your name

if at first you don't succeed recognize this as a pattern

any decent god would be laughing at you by now

it's time for a new wardrobe

the answer you most need went in the cookie to another table the cat pees on your shoes because she wants more affection

mother lied—you are in no way special

there are many new resources for those about to be audited

cheaters never win but since nothing else has worked

Before the Forest

before the forest pause
sunlight grows scarce

in that cool shade and
close pines conceal

rough beasts who already
sense your presence

everything feeds on
everything as it must

willow scrub on your oxygen
thirsty arroyo on the

flash flood and you on the
flesh of so many words

sleep together one more night
before the forest and bless

soft grass with whispers
with sugar and sweat

remember dreams and wake
in new skin without regret

a body is an elegant ruin
a kiss is two clocks ticking

in slow time for lovers
paused before the forest

who enter as one aware
one cannot return

New Sugar

wish love lust taste that

is how it happens

while traffic goes rushing

combusting lonely and metal

peel away a past

full of resistance

hands reach and release

bone from bone unhinge

shoulders so the body moves

ever upward

waiting for the plush

remembered place

a riverbed every

inch of skin

each nerve's wick

lit with sensation

dreams unraveling

the room's deep dark

until dawn through

chameleon windows spills

new sugar on her lips

Pint Poems

Pour Me

a small measure of twilight foamcapped
throat coating hurry mollify my belly
fully with a Cumbrian trailwalker's
cosmic tonic teased from a barley acre
juice brewed melopoeia a big spoon of
wind's essence flowerzest a bittersweet
thirstbane a tongueblooming stream
spilling pepper coffee chocolate and that
cool cool finish fortifying friends around
this table lifted by laughter by this harvest
of ancient amity a toast to precious mirth

Red Blessing

may you find now your lost hilarity
in the molecules of amber balm
gripped in your fist a red flood of
true food for the husk of a soul you
misplaced but must ever recover
so drink deep surrender laughter
among satyrs and saints these
companions in the infinite forest
use any language each word an
icasm striking a resonant drum
and claim this night these friends
this poem you're home warmed
again by flavor that whispers
secrets in foam and red depths

Don's Garage

door sticks needs a
shove opens on a
poor pharaoh's tomb
mostly dust rust
cobwebs greasy
tobacco tins bristle with
tacks and bolts
tape so old
it flakes away
dry-rotted wooden
tool chest
with a neat row of
bits a persistent
drill wore down
scissors still sharp
blades meet as
machined to do
unused broom
decades with its
clean quills up
ancient radio
plugged in it
sparks and smokes but
tunes twitch speaker
shelves of rags
burlap bags dangling
twine a D-Day
issued first aid kit
Don was blind
the last ten years
so nothing here
had hands on it

though the rake's tines
must have shivered
as seasons shifted
beyond smeared glass
and snow fell on his
dead wife's garden
a vague dirt patch
crabgrass claimed

Driving Home from the Airport

empty auto empty fields
sun on the grass sadder than loss

he waved goodbye she didn't see
her mind already on Parisian streets

September soon chill at night
grass tossing in the absent light

he said goodbye she didn't hear
flow of the Seine filling her ear

open highway long drive home
unlock the door nothing more

Coomb Song

inside the song a wing
a steel string a strong

breeze tinted with sweet
pea scent of forbearance

inside the lie a truth
another try a month

of silent dust-dry snow
a morning of dogsleep

inside a dream a dream
a room a grove green

midstream a roan mare
a poor prayer to gone gods

inside hunger power
the hour of knowledge of

nothingness a witness
to all this to the inner thigh

the come-cry dying drowned
in a sun-shocked coomb

inside the wind a calm
a balm a wand a vintage

saved and a nicked mug
made for such nectar

Animalia Suite

Love the Crow

no qualifiers to the caw
no modulation of the note
rending rasping chill and raw

from the bottom of his throat
bitter laugher at the dawn
cursing crows is all for naught

in the field rifle drawn
chambered shell trigger tense
aim and fire but he's gone

love the crow on the fence
no majestic bird of prey
from the carcass he will flense

flesh from bone leaving lay
a splattered sigil spelling death
on the pavement at midday

dry your eyes save your breath
you can't fly and he's in flight
roosting on a monolith

not far off but out of sight
a hacking taunting lullaby
last thing you hear at night

Thailand Black Tarantula

you stare at me alone in here
and think me delicate
though I visper vicious words
my anger and my wit

are poisonous just like the tear
I'd open in your palm
I'm agile I'll become a blur
just when you think I'm calm

and so I'll leap toward your throat
whose pulsing calls to me
the bite won't kill all pain is thrill
so come and set me free

Evilbeetle

little monster
green and copper
hateful carapace

eat the luscious
leaves leave a triumvirate
of latticed spades

colonize and likewise
skeletonize the
silver lace slung

mad over the arbor
expose its brown
bones to summer sun

I hunt you down
by dozens knock you
gorged and dull to drown

in soapy water
bucket left on hot bricks
by the larkspur

your dumb platoons
keep coming until
cold nights numb

your blunt wings and
chill gross couplings
among the chewed ruins

Flying Bear

lift off the green island
bordered by busy streets
whose ash trees are no refuge

fly away where berries
are plentiful and fish
not hard to catch if you

know the right place a rill
over black rocks then a pool
cold and clear go bear

go to that glen fly if you can
your outstretched limbs
enough for illusion of lift

Three Black Cats

the first one drags its bandaged tail
along the redbrick wall past bushes
slick with rain then leaps to the sidewalk
pads over cracks not trying to
get somewhere just hungry in chill
October air slinking here to there

the next one isn't interested in risk
crouches fierce-eyed behind
the parked police car's wheel

the last is so starved it's not a
black cat but a hole in the light
invisible at night the only time she
ventures out silent and almost floating
outlined finally under streetlamp blue
emaciated wraith no one would touch
but for that white breast patch
that hides with every step
and she pauses tail quivering

The Laboratory Pig

they keep me drunk I lie here
in the mud I eat my slop and
slurp my booze I get my shots
each afternoon I snooze
until the sun is gone
behind the laboratory hall

the research fellows dress
in fine white clothes and moving past
my pen they blur
they draw a little blood
but it don't hurt
through all this flesh anesthetized

when morning comes
with tremors in my hooves
my burnt liver swelling I'll rub
my bristled back upon the fence
and grunt from the fire in my gut and wait
for my bucket of stuff

I'm just an alcoholic pig
a laboratory hog sunken in my
artificial bog watching eucalyptus
spin listening to sows
in the next pen squealing
getting injections again

   Ten Crows

ten crows land in a beetle-killed pine
the stream keeps up its comforting
murmur but it's all lies about eternity

one bird preens a wing iridescent
sheen of black an oil slick
takes flight above a green meadow

bare brown tree casts a thin shadow
across the dirt road lengthening
as slowly as dusk gathers

one caws about the figure concealed
behind boulders at the meadow's edge
refusing any invitation to

reveal itself to enter and be fleshed
warmed by fire and nearly
alive again not a wretched ghost

the crows convulse in a dark
spiral out from tangled branches
fading away in pearled light

Twilight in Focus

dusk breeds crows
and the river's a rumor
swim into darkness to the
bottom to the stones

solar flares beget green
borealis and two coyotes
cross the wet meadow hungry
at the start of the hunt

IV

thief

Driving Monarch Pass, January

sideways snow at noon
all the dark pines frosted

past Montrose blowing thick on the
incline of Cerro Summit

and I told a friend who was
not there in my car it must be

adventure time but boy I wish
he had been there with a

joke to settle me in my seat
slow climb game of momentum

up iced grooves the only visible
pavement between schist cliffs

occluded clouds cast
chiaroscuro on white-rimmed

Blue Mesa then rising into
blindness on Monarch Pass

wheels hunting the soft edge of
traction down to Salida town

Oil and Water

two spent storms, Gulf and Pacific,
rode currents out of Mexico until
trapped in a Front Range trough

pooling in the seam between
high/low pressure
then big wind off droughted plains

drove the vapor to chilly heights
that could not hold and alchemy
unleashed a relentless deluge

steep canyons purged by
summer fires gave up their
ashy soils disgorged great

timbers and boulders in a
muddy rush side streams
turned to torrents joining

forces scouring channels
carving off slices of
highways and farm fields

down in the deeply punctured flats
twenty thousand black wells waited
and plutonium drenched benchland

outside Boulder spilled its ghosts
while taunting crows changed their
caws to frackfrackfrack and

great drums heaved crude
petroleum into the suddenly
swollen South Platte

and the St. Vrain drainage
offering now a dark drink
to the vast thirsty landscape

Canoe Canoe

1

choppy water where mudbanks narrow
smooth confluence of river and creek
gone bug's carapace hugging a stalk
these are messages ephemeral ripples
in snowmelt liquor summer released
sigils in clay but no hand no stylus
reeds and weeds slant and cross
like ogham on stone or mysterious rune
canoe canoe paddling paddling
drought-shallowed stream green and brown
straightens widens and this old boat
scrapes rock incising another striation
to ponder all winter while it leans bottom-up
against a barn's weathered wood
lines intersecting gouges and dents
each a mnemonic for noons on the flow
and nights under stars and mornings
when magpies squawked the world awake

2

fast shallow water
rock-softened shins and
cans of cold beer
on wide sandy spits
friends around a fire pit
plates of hot food and
good riddance to yesterday's
devil and tomorrow's too
give us sand between toes

and songs a river makes
give us sunset on black water
twilight when boulders seem
green beasts breaching
yellow spurge and willow
shortgrass and flotsam
choked eddies and islands
and great toppled cottonwoods
crowned with still-green leaves

Nameless Tarn

limestone boulder perched
for millennia at the pass
slowly tilted and fell urged

down the cirque its echo off
lakeglass answered by thunder
fading until finally still

and we stood on the summit of
Square Top Mountain
under thickening skies

silent with wonder nourished
from climbing August slopes
above treeline our big dog

delirious in a riot of
wildflowers white sun wind
pouring over the Divide

everything one thing
virgin forest and the raised
seabed and the nameless tarn

a dark mirror spun with
the blacker shadow
of a spiraling raptor

Daughter in a Hurricane

keep your head down when the wind
turns mean don't stand at the window

watching shop signs loosed from their
moorings careen down the street

for when windows burst that glass
can ribbon skin and blind the eyes

if a crazy man on a motorcycle makes
a late getaway then bless him

from the safety of your second floor room
and hope he's not blown off the bridge

don't clutch the cat to your chest
unless you want to learn how fear

unvelvets even a good pet's claws
the river will rise and rise and rise

and though you know the lights will
flicker and die breathe deep in those

first dark moments and become
the animal you are on an angry earth

A Good Man Goes Down

sometimes a good man will give up even
the best woman the sweet burn

of fine malt the whispered goodnight
of a drowsy child the blaze of sun on snow

yes yes sleep is a nest and
all the rest yes yes

but we only get to vanish once
to the place where all wounds cease

throbbing where the silence sounds
profound but our ears cannot hear it

so pull on the edge of the gibbous moon
until it swings wide its luminous door

fall through that hole and please let us know
whether gods await us or just the forgetting

we hang our heads down at the pub
where the alewife pours a cool cup

for Gilgamesh and for each of us
fools and saints who refuse to say

all remembering is a scribbler's jest
a charm against the emptiness

The Sand Road

for Sean

dune so steep the old dog stops
Médano Creek spills a dark braid
cold over sandburnt feet

ponderosa pine groves snag low sun
that spills copper over vanilla bark
coats deep green needles on crowns

hung with cones and ravens
high-perched hecklers hacking
taunts from windsplit silence

spin the wheels and you'll
backslide the key is to find
friction's efficient edge

drop that thing into superlow let
torque slow-chew the slope
drive while the daylight lasts

Stealing the Beautiful

this morning rising from my
last dream I was still drunk on

the sound of small waves shushing
pebbles over lakeshore shallows

I stopped to look back at the
sigils my bare feet printed

as I ran in the heavy dew
all down the length of the dock

it's good to pause and shiver at the
brink of a fast-fading vision

toe-test that glossy black
water before you leap

out over its black mirror and
submerge yourself awake

When the Woman Collapses at the Grocery Store

blood on her shin where it
nicked the shelf blood beneath
her lip where she landed
hard on aisle's polished tiles
but the muzak keeps oozing
and bright boxes of corn syrup
gleam on in row after row
frozen pizzas remain medicinal
as ever and cheesebricks plot
just as many heart attacks
apple skins still harbor a full
complement of carcinogens
and no gap opens in the
floor-to-ceiling stack of soda
sixpacks those aluminum
diabetes delivery devices

in the cool fluorescent glow
a man kneels and cradles her head
hands greasy from a garage job
his voice slow and gentle as
warm water flowing over stones
until her eyes flutter open on his
and her trembling body relaxes
the world falls away the bad
music the clamoring colors
and even the screaming child
serenading shoppers stops
so there is only this unfiltered
gift the workman's compassion

shaming all evils from this space
defeating all greed all cruelty
the sad history of hate for one
moment here now

May Morning Apotheosis

what just went rattling down your dream
a monster god or distinguished demon

a wild boar rooting among your fears
for loose roots and wild hairs

fright wig of words you couldn't comb
in a garden of grief surrounding a tomb

built so the sun through a narrow slat shines
to stir up your ashes and polish your bones

welcome at last to your apotheosis
how you achieved it is nobody's business

green grass is greener honey is sweeter
pain when it enters is hotter and cleaner

you traded your hatred for softer hands
that heal and seal your enemies' wounds

you're a man in a woman inside of a man
giving birth to a woman and man entwined

aware that all living is living to die
that to fly is to fall and to flee is to stay

poems mark the paper songs twitch the air
children replace you as if you weren't there

The Egg of Tenderness

shell so thin the light within
illuminates this darkened room

I cannot sleep the water's deep
I float and fail I rise and flail

inside my heart it breaks apart
and leaks an urge to reach and touch

white frost to trace and outer space
beyond glass blue comets pass

a frigid void where time's destroyed
so far and black so cold and bleak

midnight here my lover near
her heat her glow all I can know

Vulpine

the bleeding fox
does not limp back
to lick the leg
left in the trap